THE PRESIDENTIAL ELECTION IN 2016:

NO MORE POLITICAL HOAXES AND

TIME FOR REAL CHANGE IN AMERICA

(An Election Guide)

By

DR. ROBERT ATHANAS

This book is dedicated to all Americans working to keep the American Dream alive

CONTENTS

INTRODUCTION

The United States of America has been a great nation, a great democracy, and an empire. America has been undefeated by foreign enemies. It has the greatest fighting military machine in the world. It has been the defender and champion of liberty and democracy in the planet. With hard work, ingenuity, innovation, and entrepreneurship by its people, America has been the strongest and the richest nation on the planet.

However, it is unfortunate that the American empire is currently in decline. The American economy is in a state of continued stagnant recession. It does not appear to be able to recover from the 2008 economic calamity caused by America's crooks and greedy financiers and money men. There are many millions of Americans unemployed and underemployed. There are millions of Americans living in poverty, on welfare and food stamps. There are still millions of Americans without health insurance. In this blessed land of plenty, there are many hungry people, including children, while America's rich spend millions of dollars just for their entertainment.

The hard working middle class, which is the power engine of the United States in many respects, has been in decline and is continuously shrinking. America's middle class is struggling to make it everyday. The cherished American dream is dead for millions of Americans. America is in decay and at a crossroads. It has currently a national debt of about 18.5 trillion dollars, which is continuously growing on a daily basis. America's growing mountain of national debt is a major threat to its national security, democracy, and prosperity.

CHAPTER 1

THE 2008 ECONOMIC COLLAPSE

The 2008 economic collapse and disaster in the United States clearly showed that the American capitalist and financial system was suffering from deep and profound economic problems. It also proved that the fundamentals of the American economy were deeply flawed, and they had to be reformed to prevent any future economic collapses and disasters.The economic crisis in 2008 was primarily caused by corrupt and greedy bankers, Wall Street crooks and profiteers. The 2008 economic financial meltdown in the United States clearly proved that America's economic and financial system was taken over and highjacked by uncontrollable millionaires and billionaires who have taken over the wealth in this country. The American class of the rich has manipulated the financial system to their economic advantage. Accordingly, it was obvious in 2008 that America was at a crossroads. It was obvious the political need to clean up the financial mess caused by America's capitalists, to reform the American capitalist economic system, and to make it work for all Americans. Also, it was time to send to jail all of those who caused the American financial collapse in 2008.

THE 2008 ELECTION

In the presidential election in 2008, it was, indeed, time for real and deep changes in the American political and economic system, and America's foreign policy. In 2008, the democratic candidates for the White House were Barack Obama and Hillary Clinton. The American people rejected the recycling of the Clintons and their politics, and they voted against Hillary to be the democratic presidential nominee. The democrats voted for Obama to be the democratic nominee because they believed his promises to bring about the changes needed in the United

States.

The republican presidential nominee in 2008, John McCain, was not trusted by the American people that he would bring about the needed changes in America. The American people justifiably considered McCain to be the same recycling of President George W. Bush's failed and costly domestic and foreign policies. McCain lost the election to the first African American for the White House. The American people wisely voted for Barack Obama to be president of the United States in 2008. Despite the lack of experience by Obama, the American people trusted his message of change and hope for all Americans.   They trusted him to fix and reform the rotten, corrupt and unhealthy system of American capitalism, and to make it work for all Americans to achieve the American dream.

THE OBAMA DISAPPOINTMENT

It is true that when President Obama assumed his presidency in January 2009, the United States was in a deep financial mess and economic recession, and with high unemployment. In 2009, America was at war in both Afghanistan and Iraq and still fighting the global war on terrorism.

A   critical evaluation of the first term of President Obama clearly shows that he failed to deliver on this promises for change and hope in America. His message for a better life for the working Americans turned out to be a failed message of economic despair and hopelessness for the middle class and the poor. Despite the reported improvement of the American economy and the lowering unemployment numbers by applying phony calculation methods, it must be agreed that the working Americans are still struggling to make ends meet, and the poor are becoming more desperate. The American dream is disappearing for many millions of Americans. In particular, the

African American community has been devastated by very high unemployment and poverty. But with Obama in the White House, the rich made more money than ever before. None of the crooks or criminals who caused the 2008 economic collapse were prosecuted and jailed.

The Obamacare health system, which is an achievement on the part of President Obama, has failed to meet its objectives, and it has not been very successful. There are still millions of Americans uninsured, and the insurance health premiums have been significantly increased on the working Americans. The health cost crisis in America has not been resolved.

Many millions of Americans are poor and on food stamps. America's national debt has reached about 18.5 trillion dollars, which is more than double than that of the George W. Bush presidency. This growing mountain of national debt leads the country to financial collapse and bankruptcy.

During his first term, President Obama was not successful in his foreign policy pursuits. Despite his decision to withdraw the American forces from both Afghanistan and Iraq, his policies with respect to Iraq and Afghanistan have not been successful. Iraq has become a failed and divided state with enormous domestic terrorism. In Afghanistan, there is a major resurgence by the Taliban and their movement of terror. Obama's Arab spring policies have been a failure, which caused the creation of failed states, such as Libya. His policy approach to the Syrian civil war and conflict has been a colossal disaster. This failure created gaps and the environment which has led to the creation of the ISIS terror group, and its barbaric atrocities in the region. In conclusion, the first term of President Obama turned out to be a disappointment to many Americans.

THE 2012 ELECTION AND THE ONE PERCENT

In the 2012 election, with the Obama disappointment to so

many Americans, anybody running against his failed promises for change would have won. Only someone from the 1% class of the rich Americans would have lost such an election, and this a person was Mitt Romney, the republican presidential nominee. In 2012, Obama did not run on his accomplishments because he did not have much to say to the American people. But Obama, with the help of the sold out American mass media, was able to win the election with the 1% rich trick and the 47% of whining Americans statement by Romney, which was a huge gift of re-election to President Obama.

Romney, as a multi-millionaire, and as a member of the American class of the 1% rich, was not trusted by the American people that he would care for the working people and the poor. In particular, his statement that 47% of Americans are whining, receiving government benefits and other entitlements, and they do not pay taxes was devastating to his presidential bid. By his own mouth, he offended many millions of Americans who have worked hard to get their small social security checks, and many of them, including republicans, decided to stay home than vote for Romney. Thus, Obama won by default. In any case, the American people gave to him a second chance to keep his promises for change and to make America a better place for all, and not only the rich.

However, an overview of his second term as president, Obama failed again to do better. He failed to change America for the better for all Americans. He failed to show leadership and to achieve a fair and just American economic system to benefit all Americans, and not the top 1%, or 2% rich. His domestic policies have largely failed. The American economy is stagnant, and it has not recovered from the 2008 economic disaster for which Obama was elected to fix. Many millions of Americans are unemployed, underemployed and giving up seeking employment. Millions of Americans are poor and on food stamps. The American middle class is gradually disappearing.

However, the rich with Obama in the White House have become richer. The same crooks are still in charge of the corrupt and rotten American banking and financial system.They are still free and immune from prosecution and from going to jail for causing America's financial collapse in 2008. The crooks of America's financial system are still inflating more bubbles in the Wall Street casino and in the other sectors of the American economy, which will cause the next devastating economic disaster in America. There is still the same political corruption in Washington, D.C. America's rich have bought and control the U.S. Congress with their money contributions. There is still deep division on Capitol Hill with no regard towards the needs of the American people. The members of Congress are well off financially and many of them are millionaires. But the American people are still left out in the cold.

With respect to his foreign policy in the second term, President Obama has failed again. The situation in Iraq, Afghanistan and generally in the Middle East is in a state of disaster. His approach towards ISIS, the most ruthless and barbaric terrorist middle east group, is disastrous. His inept interventions in Ukraine have caused a new Cold War with Russia. Let us not forget that Russia is the only country with a massive nuclear weapons arsenal capable of making America a land of radioactive waste in the event of a nuclear conflict with Russia. It is in the national security interest of the United States and Russia to reestablish strong and lasting relations for their own sake and the sake of global peace and security. America and Russia have more common interests in fighting together terror groups such as ISIS and the islamic fundamentalism in the world. Both Russia and the United States must form a new coalition and common front to fight side by side and defeat ISIS and the evils of the rising islamic fundamentalism and terror. Both countries need each other in this long struggle.

President Obama was given twice a historic chance by the American people to make America a better place for all Americans. He had a unique chance in view of the 2008 economic crisis and financial mess to make capitalism work and benefit all Americans, and not the rich. Unfortunately, with Obama in the White House, the gap between the rich and poor grew even further, and poverty grew more in America.

To the disappointment of many Americans, President Obama failed to deliver on his promises for change in America. Indeed, President Obama lost a unique and dynamic opportunity to create economic opportunity for the poor and hard working Americans, and to eliminate poverty in America. He failed to get America's filthy rich to pay their fair share of taxes, which could be used to achieve a more fair distribution of wealth in this country. He failed to set in motion the political and legal process to close the growing wide income gap between the poor and the rich in America. With Obama in the White House, the rich got richer than ever before, the poor got devastated, the working people are struggling to make it, and America got broke with a mountain of national debt. It is no wonder why the crooks who caused the economic collapse and disaster in America in 2008 did not go to jail, and they still are in control and power in America. President Obama is a good, compassionate and caring person. He tried to bring change to America. Nevertheless, it is not enough to be a nice person, and try to change Washington because it is doomed to fail. To change Washington, you need dynamic leadership.

Let us face it, the class of the 1% rich control and rule this country, and the rest 99% of us are trying to make it every day. Let us also understand that all American presidents and members of the U.S. Congress belong to the same club of the rich and the well off financially. It is naive to continue to expect them to help the ordinary and hard working Americans, and to feel compassion for America's poor and unfortunate. There is a cozy relationship between America's politicians and America's rich. This relationship has downgraded the great American democracy, and it has led this great nation to decline and to be financially broke. It is time for real change in America and nothing less. We should not allow any more political hoaxes in America. Simply, we cannot afford it anymore.

CHAPTER 2

THE 2016 PRESIDENTIAL ELECTION: NO MORE BUSHES,

NO MORE CLINTONS

In 2008, Hillary Clinton was defeated in the democratic primary in her political effort to be the nominee of the democratic party for the presidency. The Clinton political machine and their connections suffered a devastating blow and defeat by an African American man, Barack Obama, who promised to bring change to America.

In 2008, the American people rejected the effort by the Clintons, Bill and Hillary, to go back to the White House. Indeed, the American people wisely decided to defeat the Clintons and to prevent them from returning to the White House. In essence, the American people were fed up with the Clintons and their recycling in America's politics and power. They said no more for Clintons returning to the White House.

Currently, Hillary Clinton in running again to be the nominee of the democratic party for the presidency in the 2016 election. Obviously, this is one more effort by the Clintons to return to the White House in 2016. It is also obvious that the Clintons are addicted to the political power of the American presidency and politics.

There is no need to remind to the American people the stories, affairs, and scandals of Bill Clinton while in the White House. But it is important to remind to the American people that Bill Clinton's questionable economic policies together with the Federal Reserve, and his failure to regulate the American bankers played a significant role in creating an economic bubble, which caused the 2008 economic disaster in America. It is also important to point out that if Hillary Clinton is elected to the presidency in 2016, Bill Clinton will be back in the White House and in charge, and believe me, you don't want Bill back and roaming around in the White House.

Now, let us talk about Hillary and why she must be defeated in her second effort to be elected to the presidency in 2016. First of all, Hillary as the first lady, going through the trauma of Bill's affairs and scandals while in the White House, was not able to achieve anything of importance to help the hard working people and the poor of America.

As a former U.S. Senator, Hillary did not accomplish anything of significance to help the American people improve their lives. Moreover, as a former Secretary of State, Hillary failed again to show the required leadership as America's top diplomat in the world arena. As former secretary of state, Hillary failed to resolve any international problems, conflicts and crises. By the time she left the state department, she left behind her a world in turmoil, crisis and conflict. She failed to reset relations with Russia, she failed to resolve the middle east conflict, and she generally failed to promote America's interests abroad. The American people cannot forget the Benghazi tragedy and massacre of Americans while Hillary was the Secretary of State.

In conclusion, Hillary's tenure as the head of the state department was a waste of time and taxpayers' money. There is not even one major accomplishment that she achieved as secretary of state. Hillary's appointment by President Obama in the state department was a bad decision and investment. As secretary of state, Hillary simply wasted the taxes of the American people for her aimless travels and expenses abroad. In particular, the currently reported problems of Hillary's e-mail private server and the official Department of State e-mails on it are a serious matter. Apparently, the only thing that Hillary was successful in doing as secretary of state was erasing thousands of e-mails from her private e-mail server. The American people must be deeply concerned about Hillary's ambition to the be the next president.

Generally speaking, in this country nobody is above the law, and everybody must play according to the rules. Even the most rich and the most politically powerful must obey the law as the ordinary citizens do. The American people must stand against dirty political tricks, and lack of transparency. The American people must support honesty, and transparency in the political process before they make their political choices during elections.

The powerful Clinton political machine and its connections to the rich and the sold out American major mass media will try to fool the American voters to make Hillary the next president in 2016, and thus to send both Clintons back to the White House. They will try to get their vote by brainwashing them that Hillary cares for the hard working ordinary citizens, the minorities and the poor, that she feels their pain and suffering, and if elected president, she will help them out and make their lives better.

The Americn voters must not allow themselves to be fooled by the Clintons and by other politicians and their phony politics. The Clintons are rich and powerful for themselves. They have become a money making machine and multimillionaires. They are not poor and desparate like so many other Americans. The Clintons do not really deeply care about the poor and hard working Americans. The Clintons cannot really identify themselves with the poor and the working class of Americans who are trying to make ends meet everyday. The Clintons belong to the class of rich Americans. But to serve their political ambitions, the Clintons continue the same litany that they feel the pain of the poor and hard working Americans. It is hard for rational people to believe them anymore. They simply try to get your vote to have Hillary and Bill returning in the White House again as the comeback kids, and then forget about you.

Hillary makes nice speeches that she cares about women and their issues. It is obvious that if Hillary is the democratic nominee and if she gets the womens' vote she will be elected president in 2016. But Hillary is a politician, and the American women must be careful with their political choice and vote in 2016. It must be pointed out that the American women must not forget that it has been reported that,while in the U.S. Senate, Hillary paid her women staffers less than the male staffers.

The American people must realize that all politicians, no matter how nice and charming they really are or trying to be during elections, do not care about anybody else except themselves and their ambitions. They are thirsty for political power and wealth.

Accordingly, in 2016, it is time for dynamic and revolutionary political decisions and choices in America for real change. The American people must defeat the Clinton political machine, and they must vote to say no more to Clintons in the White House. The American people must not be fooled, and they must reject the recycling of the Clintons in the White House.

As far as the Jeb Bush candidacy for the White House in 2016 is concerned, just remember his mother, Barbara, when she said that we had enough Bushes in the White House. When Barbara says that we had enough Bushes, the American voters must listen to her advice. The Bushes are a powerful and wealthy family of presidents, and governors. The Bushes believe that they have royal rights to the White House throne. The Bush political machine and their rich friends and supporters will try to make Jeb the next president in 2016. Their efforts must be defeated by the American people.

The American people must not forget that the older Bush, George H.W., as president, failed to play a dynamic role in the creation of a peaceful new global order with the end of the cold war. He also presided over the worst economic recession in the United States since the Jimmy Carter presidency.

With respect to George W. Bush, the American people must not forget that he was president during the 9/11 tragic terrorist attack on America. He committed strategic blunders with the invasion of Iraq in 2003, which caused the death of thousands of American soldiers and left thousands wounded, and it cost trillions of dollars to America. Also, George W. presided over the 2008 economic collapse in America. Accordingly, it is obvious that Jeb will not be any different from the failed presidencies of his father and brother. The American voters must defeat the Bush political machine to put Jeb in the White House in 2016. It is time for the American people to say enough, and no more Bushes in the White House in 2016. If Jeb is elected in 2016, it is hard to believe that his presidency would be any different from that of his father and his brother. Don't expect better. Since they like the oil business, the Bushes usually go to war in the oil rich Middle East with America's children.

REJECT AND DEFEAT ALL POLITICTIANS FOR PRESIDENT IN 2016

Politicians cannot be trusted. After the double disappointment by Obama, the American voters must reject and defeat all politicians running as candidates for the White House in 2016. All candidates currently running for the presidency in 2016 with both democratic and republican parties are politicians, who must be rejected and defeated by the American voters. Currently, with the democratic party, Hillary Clinton, Bernie Sanders and Martin O'Malley are running for the White House 2016 election. I have already discussed the reasons for which the American voters must defeat Hillary and say no to more Clintons in the White House.

As far as U.S. Senator Bernie Sanders is concerned, it must be pointed out that he has been a Washington career politician since 1990. Despite his efforts to persuade the American public otherwise, Senator Sanders is still a politician who cannot be trusted to deliver on his promises to change Washington, D.C.

We heard the same things and even better things and promises from Obama before and got disappointed in him twice. Accordingly, the American voters must defeat Bernie Sanders' presidential bid.

As far as the presidential bid of Martin O'Malley is concerned, it must be pointed out that he is a former Maryland governor. As a governor, he did not accomplish anything of significance. He imposed so many taxes on the people of Maryland. O'Malley has a tax addiction. As governor, he was not able to bring prosperity to the state of Maryland, to create jobs, and bring in businesses. The American people must reject and defeat him as another politician having the ambition to be president. His politics have failed the people of Maryland. He must be rejected and defeated.

If the current Vice President, Joe Biden, runs for the presidency in 2016, the American people must not forget that Joe is a career Washington politician. He has been in Washington for more than 40 years. He has not been able to accomplish anything of significance for the American people. Joe has been addicted to the Washington power. He still has the ambition to climb to the highest office in the land, the White House. Despite his slogans and political rhetoric, Joe does not care too much about the other ordinary and hard working Joes and Janes of America. He currently complains that the income inequality hurts the country. But Joe has been in Washington, D.C. for more than 40 years and still he did not do anything to fix it. It is time for Joe to go back home and not to the White House. Joe was not able to help the American people for the last more than four decades. How many more chances does he need? Even if we give him one more chance, he will not do anything substantial for us. It is time for Joe to go back home.

Currently, the candidates running with the republican party for the White House in 2016 include: U.S. senator Marco Rubio, U.S. senator Ted Cruz, New Jersey governor, Chris Christie, Winsconsin governor, Scott Walker, former Arkansas governor Mike Huckabee, U.S. senator Lindsey Graham, U.S. senator Rand Paul, Ohio governor, John Kasich, Carly Fiorina, Ben

Carson, Donald Trump, former U.S senator Rick Santorum, and former New York governor, George Pataki.

With the exception of Fiorina, Trump and Ben Carson, all other republican candidates for president in 2016 are all politicians, who are part of the problem and not part of the solution to America's political and economic problems. Despite their fat promises for change and fat statements that they are a different kind of politicians, that they care about the American people and the direction of the country, do not believe them, and do not trust them. They are a bunch of ambitious politicians who do not really care about the hard working Americans and their economic needs and problems. They have been in Washington, D.C. and they have not accomplished anything of significance for the American people and the country. Simply, they try to say that they are for change to get your vote to satisfy their poltical ambition to reside in the White House. All of them must be rejected and defeated by the American people.

With respect to Fiorina running for the White House in 2016, she is a business woman and she was a former CEO of Hewlett-Packard. She lost her bid in 2010 to be a U.S. senator from California. Otherwise, she believes to win the White House in 2016 while she was not even able to get elected as a senator.

Dr. Ben Carson is a retired distinguished pediatric neurosurgeon. He is a man of careful and measured words. He has no political experience. But he is the only African American so far running for president in 2016. Despite his current elevation in the polls, unfortunately, many Americans cannot forget their double disappointment in President Obama. America is, unfortunately, a big patient at this time and it needs a dynamic surgeon to restore its health, glory and greatness for all Americans. Dr. Carson does not appear to be decisive and dynamic to deal with America's problems. If Dr. Carson is elected president in 2016, I hope that he does not follow the same path of unkept promises for change as Predisent Obama did to our disappointment.

As far as Trump's presidential bid is concerned, Trump is the only businessman so far running with the republican party for the White House. He is a real estate businessman and a multibillionaire who has the ambition to be in America's most precious and cherished real estate, the White House. Let us be serious about it. Trump is a real estate tycoon and multibillionaire. He belongs to the top 1% rich. The last multimillioanaire who ran for the White House in 2012 was Mitt Romney and he lost. Let us see if the American hard working middle class, the minorities and the poor people will fall this time for a multibillionaire in 2016 for the White House, if Trump is finally the nominee, or if they will fire him.

CHAPTER 3

TIME FOR REAL CHANGE IN 2016

It is obvious that the current runners for the White House in 2016 are all politicians, except Carly Fiorina, Dr. Ben Carson, and the multibillionaire, Donald Trump. These politicians cannot be trusted and believed by the American people. Despite their fat promises for change and their statements that they care for the ordinary American people, their promises are hollow and hard to believe. Simply, their promises are another political hoax perpetrated by politicians on the American people every four years. We got all these nice promises from Obama before, and now we know what we got. Don't fall for these phony promises for the 2016 election. They will not keep their promises. After all, it is the politicians and their rich backers and supporters, who have caused America's decline, and they have let the American people down.

If in 2016 we make the same foolish mistake to send politicians back to Washington, D.C. in the White House and Congress, we should not expect that our lives will be better,and Amercia will be strong again. For sure, the rich will continue to have their politicians in Washington, D.C. to care for them and to make them richer. But who will we have to care for the hard working Americans in Washington in 2016? Probably nobody.

It is time to reject the Washington, D.C. political culture, and failed and bankrupt politics which have harmed America and its people. It is time to end and outlaw the control of the Washington politicians and politics by the rich. It is time for the American people to wake up, to come out from their political apathy, and to begin a new and dynamic grassroots campaign to take America back from the control of the corrupt politics, the crooks and the filthy rich.

In 2016, it is time for all Americans to unite and to put an end to the two party political tyranny in America. Both democrats and republicans are the same, and both have led America to decline, and they have failed the American people. It is time to throw them out and fail them too. America is at a crossroads and at peril. It is time for the people to clean the mess and corruption in Washington, and to restore America's power and its promise. We have to put an end to Washington's career politicians, lobbyists and political parasites of all sorts.

It is unacceptable and unpatriotic for the American people to have allowed to continue for so long the failed politicians and their phony politics, which have ruined this great nation. It is totally absurd that in America with about 320 million people that we cannot find a few good, honest, competent and smart people to send to Washington, D.C. to serve us and the country.

In today's America, the rich, the lobbyists, the special domestic and foreign power interests and the corrupt political culture in Washington control the entire democratic poltical process. In today's America, only people with money, or supported by people with money, can afford to get elected either to the White House or Congress. It is difficult for any ordinary citizen with no money and financial support to run and to be elected to a federal office. Indeed, in today's America, the rich and the career politicians and politics have highjacked the American electoral process, and they have greatly undermined the American democracy.

In view of the 2016 election, we must not commit the same foolish mistake of sending to Washington the same career politicians who are only the representatives of the rich and powerful and not of the American people. We must not allow the continuation of the same corrupt politics, which have let the American people down, and they have led a great nation to decline, and they have undercut and undermined the great American democracy. It is a great patriotic duty to take America back, and to rebuild a great and fair America again for all Americans.

In America, there is the corrupt system of the two party political tyranny, which has led the country to the point of bankruptcy, and it has led the American people down. Both democratic and republican parties are the same, and they have managed for too long to alternate in power and control in Washington both in Congress and the White House. Both democrats and republicans are controlled by the rich and they serve the interests of the rich, and not the interests and needs of the working Americans and the poor. The republicans simply want to make the rich richer. The democrats pretend to care to help the middle class, the minorities and the poor. However, the politics of the democratic party and their promises to the minorities and the poor have been a hoax for a long time. The minorities have been wasting their vote by voting for either democrats or republicans.

Democrats do not really care too much about the working and the poor. They only want to fool them over and over with their phony promises to get their votes and to stay in power in Washington. Both parties are part of the same problem in Washington and not part of the solution. Both parties are the recycling of the same old corrupt and failed politics in Washington. Both democratic and republican parties are failed parties, and they have failed America and its people. In 2016, it is time to end the failed and corrupt regime and tyranny of the two party political power and control system in America. At least in 2016, the American people must begin the process to end the corrupt and phony politics in Washington played by both democrats and republicans for too long.

It will be, indeed, foolish for the American voters to vote for the democratic or republican politicians and candidates for the White House and Congress in 2016. Don't expect any real change in Washington if the democrats or republicans are in power in 2016. Expect more economic decline and more political corruption.

The independent and non party affiliated voters in America are a huge and power voting block which decides the presidential and congressional elections in this country.

However, the independents are politically homeless in this country, and they carry favor to both democrats and republicans by voting for their candidates. In this way, the independents elect both democrat and republican politicians and thus maintain the two party regime in control in Washington without any prospects for real political change. In a sense, the independents live in a world of political illusion. They waste their vote by voting for the democratic and republican candidates, which have created this huge mess in this country. As long as the independents continue to vote for either democrats or republicans in federal elections, the realistic expectation for change is close to zero, and thus they really fail themselves and the country.

A STRATEGIC POLITICAL ACTION PLAN FOR REAL CHANGE, REFORM AND RENEWAL IN 2016

There are currently about 220 million eligible voters in America. However, in the 2012 presidential election, only about 126 million voted, which is only about 57% of the eligible voters in the country. Apparently, there is a serious disease of political apathy, ignorance and indifference of many millions of American voters. Many millions of Americans do not vote because they are fed up and sickened by the same old corrupt politics of Washington and the constant failure for change. So they prefer staying home than showing up and voting. If the overwhelming majority of Americans voted in elections, they would have been able to throw all political bums and junkies out of office in Washington. They would have ended the political culture and corruption in Washington, and they would have made real and deep changes in America to make it a better place for all Americans. It is not only a constitutional right to vote, but it is also a great patriotic duty in our constitutional democracy. To keep the American democracy alive and to maintain our freedoms, all Americans have to vote in elections. Do not allow the rich, the corrupt and the sold out media to brainwash Americans and trick them to vote for certain people they want to promote in elections for federal offices in Washington, D.C. If we allow them to brainwash and fool us, eventually the United States and the rest of us will pay the price for making the wrong political choices.

It is time for the American public to be politically educated and active. Americans should not allow themselves to be fooled and brainwashed by the media in making their own political choices during elections. Only an educated and actively involved American electorate can put an end to political hoaxes, false political promises, and to bring the changes needed to make America and its capitalist system work for all Americans and not the rich ones. It is time for the American electorate to wake up and to vote for political choices, which make America great again and fair to all Americans. In this age of rich internet information and other social media, it is totally unacceptable for many millions of American voters to allow themselves to be manipulated by the media on making their political choices in elections. It is unacceptable that many millions of Americans prefer to stay home and not vote, and thus show their dissatisfaction with the political candidates and the political system. This is the wrong approach. Americans have a constitutional right to vote and they must exercise it. They must not allow a minority of voters in America to determine the future course of the country.

America is a great country with millions of hard working, smart and honest people. It is unacceptable that in this country of about 320 million people, we cannot find a few smart and honest people to send to Washington and throw out the do nothing career politicians, and political junkies addicted to power and money.

Even if some good, smart and honest Americans are willing to run for the U.S. Congress and the White House, and to make real changes in Washington and in America, they, unfortunately, do not have the money and the resources to run their election campaigns. The corrupt political system in Washington has established a financial contribution system, which benefits the Washington career politicians and those connected to the rich. Ordinary people willing to serve the country and make a difference cannot run for federal office simply because they have no money. It takes millions of dollars for someone to run and be elected to the U.S. Congress, and probably more than a billion dollars for the White House. Simply, the rich have found the way to buy elections and influence in Washington, D.C. with their money.

It is time to reform the federal law on financial contributions to candidates for federal elections. The money donations to candidates running for federal office by PACs and SuperPACs, and special groups and foreign power entities must be outlawed and criminalized. Only small money donations not exceeding $100 by individuals must be allowed. The adoption of this proposed reform will put an end to rich and powerful electing presidents and congressmen with their huge money donations. This will unleash the power of the vast majority of Americans to send presidents and congressmen to Washington, D.C. to serve the American people and not only the rich. The adoption of this proposal will guarantee deep and real change in America's politics as usual. America must wake up. The presidents are rich, the congressmen are all well off, and many of them are rich and getting richer. The rich are getting richer. However, the American people are getting poorer, and this not fair.

GRASSROOTS POLITICAL REVOLUTION

It is still time for at least making the beginning for a new dynamic and revolutionary grassroots campaign to change America's old and corrupt politics. At a grassroots level, all Americans must be involved to choose candidates for the White House and Congress in the 2016 election and afterwards, who have nothing to do with the Washington political corruption and mess. There are at least many thousands of smart, good, honest and hard working Americans willing to serve the American people if we support them and send them to Washington.

However, we have to make sure that they will agree to term limits. Nobody in Washington should serve no more than eight years in Congress as the president serves in the White House. It is, indeed, insane to allow congressmen to serve for several decades and even more than half a century in congress while they are doing nothing for the American people. They must also pledge to pass constitutional amendments and laws to allow the recall of congressmen and even presidents for not keeping their promises to the American people. They must agree to pass laws to balance the federal budget in a fair manner, and to begin to pay off gradually the huge national debt. The American people must have the first and the last word on whom to send to Washington, and whom to recall from Washington and send them back home.

THE AMERICAN MONEY PIE AND THE AMERICAN DREAM

Let us discuss some simple facts about America's wealth and the American economy. America is a blessed and wealthy nation. In 2015, the GDP of the United States is about 18 trillion dollars. Currently, the United States has a population of about 320 million people. The current American labor force is about 157 million people. There are currently about 148 million fully employed in the United States, and about 9 million of Americans unemployed or underemployed. Yet, there many millions of Americans, capable of work, but not working, or seeking employment.

The current median income in the United States is about $50,000 for 123 million of households. The rest of the working Americans earn a lot less. However, in the United States the top 1% rich own more than 40% of America's wealth. The top 10% of the upper middle class in the country own about 12% of its wealth. Thus, the top 10% in this country own about 90% of its wealth. The rest of the ordinary and hard working Americans own only the remaining 10% of America's wealth. This is not just and fair at all. In the United States only about 30 million Americans have the money and the wealth and the means to live and enjoy the American dream in all of its glory.

The rest of about 300 million Americans are struggling to make it everyday. The hard working middle class in America is loosing ground, is shrinking and disappearing. There about 40 million people in this country who live in poverty, on welfare and food stamps. There still millions of Americans without health insurance. There are millions of children in this nation of plenty who are hungry. It is unfortunate that the American dream is dying, and it has been already dead for many millions of hard working, decent, honest and patriotic Americans. The realities of the American dream are unlimited for America's rich. The potential to reach the American dream for ordinary citizens is increasingly hard.

Let us be clear that the hard working Americans are people who are not asking for welfare assistance and handouts by the government. They are simply asking for jobs, decent jobs with decent pay, and job security. They are asking for realistic opportunities to live decent lives and to reach the Amrican dream. To have a house in America is a human right and it should not be a dream. To have a a decent income to raise and to support your family and live a decent life through hard work is a right and not a dream.

It is, indeed, unacceptable that the 1% rich Americans own more wealth than the rest 90% in this nation. This simple math clearly shows the huge income inequality between the rich and the working people in America. Yet, we have Donald Trump, a multibillionaire, who keeps saying that he is really rich while running for the peoples' house in 2016, the White House. Let us see how the hard working Americans, the minorities and the poor, who are struggling to make everyday, will appreciate his White House run.

It is time in America for real economic reforms. Do not expect any changes in Washington to help the working Americans, and the poor if we continue sending to Washington the same old political culture. It is time to share the American money pie in a fair way for all Americans. The insanity and foolishness that only

1% rich owns more wealth than the rest of us is got to stop, and it is got to change. To achieve this strategic goal, we need deep changes in Washington with political and economic reforms. We need to elect and send to Washington a new generation of decent, hard working, honest and caring Americans to reverse America's decline and to make it great again and fair to all Americans and not the rich ones. Let us make capitalism work for all Ameicans and not the few rich.

Let us be clear that communism was a failed totalitarian, suppressive, inhumane and dictatorial system. Socialist is also a bad political system. However, it should be agreed that also capitalism has become a corrupt and sick system, which makes the rich richer, the poor poorer, and the people in the middle struggling to make ends meet. It is time to return to a reformed capitalist system of free market and enterprise where the rich and the corporations pay their fair taxes without providing them with any more corporate welfare.

It is time to start the strategic reindustrialization of the United States. America cannot continue to outsource its jobs to cheap labor countries, and to become only a service economy. America must become a new power house of advanced heavy and light industries of new products. It is time for America's rich to answer to this patriotic call and strategic plan to reindustrialize America again, to bring their money back to America from China and other parts of the world, and to create decent jobs with decent pay in the United States again.The rich Americans who invest in this plan must be rewarded with incentives and tax benefits.

Let America's rich and the entrepreneurs rebuild America and provide to the American people decent jobs with decent pay. If they do that, reward them. If they keep investing in China or India or other parts of the world to maximize their profit with exploiting the cheap labor abroad, then they should be taxed heavily in the United States. If they break the law and they steal peoples' money, they must go to jail, and take away their wealth, which they stole from others. The American people

Must not forget the economic catastrophe in 2008 from which the country cannot recover. Let the rich make money in the United States by returning to the healthy principles and practices of capitalism, which made America a great nation. But we need to make sure that the American money pie and the American wealth is shared in a fair manner by all Americans. To achieve these goals, we need to change Washington and its corrupt political culture.

CONCLUSION

The 2016 presidential election is very critical for the direction of the country. The choice to make a difference and to make America great again for all Americans belongs only to the American people. If we allow the political mess and political hoaxes to continue in the same way, then we allow, as a people, the continuation of America's decline and our own downfall.

It is time to end the corrupt political culture in Washington, D.C., and to clean up their mess and the mess they caused to America. We must end the political incompetence and foolishness prevailing in the nation's capitol. In 2016, we need to elect a new generation of smart, competent, honest, hard working and caring leaders. The failed old and new career politicians must be sent back home to get real jobs like all other Americans.

We cannot afford to continue the same failed politics which have led America to decline and to the point of near bankruptcy. We have to reverse America's decay and to renew and restore its power and greatness. It is time to make deep political and economic reforms to guarantee that the rich will pay their fair share of taxes, and the rest of the working Americans will get a fair share of the American money pie. Let us ensure that capitalism works and benefits all Americans, and not just the top 1%.

America and its empire has not been defeated by outside enemies and forces. Let us not make the historical mistake to allow the decline and final collapse of America by inside political and economic corruption, incompetence and lack of smart leadership. Let us end the political apathy in America and ensure that all Americans will participate in the political process and vote in elections to make a difference with intelligent choices.